I0017045

Exam Dumps

PSM Professional Scrum Master II Exam Prep and Dumps

SCRUM PSM II Guidebook
Updated questions

Copyright © 2023 by Byte Books

All rights reserved. No part of this book may be reproduced, stored in a retrieval system, or transmitted in any form or by any means, electronic, mechanical, photocopying, recording, or otherwise, without the prior written permission of the publisher, except for brief quotations embodied in critical reviews and certain other noncommercial uses permitted by copyright law.
For permissions inquiries or to request permission to use specific content from this book, please contact the publisher at:

Any individual or entity found infringing upon the copyright of this book will be liable for damages and legal expenses incurred as a result of such infringement.
While every effort has been made to ensure the accuracy and completeness of the information contained in this book, the author and the publisher assume no responsibility for errors or omissions or for any consequences arising from the use of the information contained herein.

Cover design and layout by Lara McCarthy.

First Edition: Aug 2023

Welcome to Byte Books: Your Path to Exam Success!

At Byte Books, we are dedicated to helping aspiring professionals achieve their career goals through comprehensive exam certification guides and practice questions. We understand that exams can be daunting, and the path to success may seem challenging. That's why we're here to provide you with the knowledge, confidence, and support you need to excel in your chosen field.

Our Mission: Empowering Your Success

Our mission is simple yet powerful: to empower your success. We believe that with the right study materials and guidance, you can overcome any exam hurdle and unlock new opportunities for personal and professional growth. At Byte Books, we go the extra mile to curate top-notch resources that cater to a wide range of certification exams, covering various industries and professions.

QUESTION 1

An organization has just hired you as a new Scrum Master to help them transition their teams from their current traditional process to Scrum. The teams are currently structured to specialize in a single function. This is also known as component teams where a team would only address a single layer (i.e. design, frontend, backend, database, testing, etc.). You've introduced the concept of cross-functional teams where all the skills needed to produce business functionality, from end to end, are inside of a single team.

What should you keep in mind when transitioning from siloed teams to cross-functional teams? (Choose two.)

A. It is easier to compare the performance between cross-functional teams in order to identify to which teams to assign tasks and which teams need additional coaching.
B. Newly formed teams will need time to stabilize before reaching their peak performance. During the initial stages of forming, performance will suffer and productivity may be low, although even then delivery of business value is still likely to increase.
C. Without feature teams, you cannot do Scrum. Postpone Scrum adoption until the teams are reorganized in feature teams.
D. People from the different layers and components will need time to become accustomed to working and delivering unified functionality together as one Scrum Team thus productivity may suffer.

Explanation:

Forming a team takes time, and members often go through recognizable stages as they change from being a collection of strangers to a united group with common goals. Bruce Tuckman's Forming, Storming, Norming, and Performing model describes these stages. When you understand it, you can help your new team becomeeffective more quickly.

QUESTION 2

Paul is a Product Owner for multiple products. Each product is allocated a dedicated Scrum Team and a set budget. Based on the average velocity of a previousproduct release, Paul had estimated a new product to take 9 Sprints to complete. The average velocity of the previous product release was 50 completed units of work per Sprint. Over the first 3 Sprints, the Development Team reported an average velocity of 40 completed units per Sprint, while not fully completing the required integration tests. The Development Team estimates that integration testing would require additional effort to make the increments shippable. The Development Team is unsure if the required velocity is achievable.

What is the most effective way to recover?

A. In the next Sprints, the Development Team strives to make the selected work as close to 'done' as possible and at the minimum 90% completed. Any undonework is divided into new Product Backlog Items that will be deferred to the last Sprint in order to maintain stable velocity.

B. The Development Team informs Paul that the progress he has perceived to date is not correct. The Increment is not releasable. They give Paul their estimate of the effort it would take to get the previous work 'done', and suggest doing that work first before proceeding with new features. The team also re-estimates the effort to make the remaining Product Backlog items 'done', including all integration effort. In the end, it is Paul's call to continue the project or to cancel.

C. The Scrum Master will manage the Sprint Backlog and assign work to the Development Team members to ensure maximum utilization of each member. He/shewill keep track of unused resources so that it does not impact the budget. Unused budget can be allocated for additional Sprints if needed.

D. The Scrum Master sets the open work aside to be performed in one or more release Sprints. They remind Paul to find funding for enough Release Sprints inwhich this remaining work can be done. Up to one release Sprint per three development Sprints may be required. It is Paul's role to inform users and stakeholders of the impact on the release date.

Explanation:
Scrum is founded on empirical process control and asserts that knowledge comes from experience and making decisions based on what is known. Scrum employsan iterative, incremental approach to optimize predictability and control risk. At the end of every Sprint, an increment of 'done' work must be available in order to inspect and adapt accordingly.

QUESTION 3

Steven, the Scrum Master, is approached by one of the Development Team members saying that they are not completing regression tests for all of the work they are performing to the level defined in the Definition of Done. They have discussed this with the Product Owner and decided to remove regression testing from the Definition of Done.

Which two actions are the most appropriate for Steven to take? (Choose two.)

A. Reject the decision as the long term maintainability of the product will be negatively impacted by modifying the Definition of Done.
B. Accept the decision as a mutual agreement has been made between the Development Team and the Product Owner.
C. Ask the Development Team and the Product Owner what problem they are trying to solve by altering the Definition of Done and removing regression testing from it. In what ways will this decision impact transparency and quality?
D. Ask the Development Team and the Product Owner if they are still able to produce potentially shippable product increments by altering the Definition of Done?

Explanation:

As a servant/leader, the Scrum Master facilitates conversations through open ended questions in order to help the team members make the best possible decisions according to what is known at the time. He/she does not approve or reject team decisions but ensures the team stays within the boundaries of the Scrum framework.

QUESTION 4

At the end of the eighth Sprint, the internal sponsors are upset and angry with the progress of the product being built. The current state of the product is not as expected and will require additional Sprints and more budget than originally anticipated at the start of the project.

What factors may have led to this? (Choose three.)

A. The Product Owner has not been engaging with sponsors frequently enough and has not been kept aware of the overall progress of the project.
B. The sponsors haven't been using the Sprint Reviews to actively engage, and inspect and evaluate progress.
C. The scope changes have not been tracked adequately and the change request process has not been followed properly.
D. The stakeholders have not been using the Daily Scrum effectively to track the Development Team's progress.
E. The Scrum Master has not ensured transparency.
F. The project plan proposed to the sponsors at the start of the project followed stringently.

Explanation:

One of the principles of agility includes working closely with business people. In order to manage stakeholder expectation, there must be open communication (through collaboration and transparency) throughout the project cycle. This maximizes alignment, helps with making business decisions, and reduces risk.

Although, the Scrum Guide does not directly state that the Scrum Master is responsible for ensuring transparency it is implicit. The Scrum Master is responsible for the process in which Scrum is adopted and enacted. Scrum is founded on empiricism and the Scrum Master helps those inside and outside the team work in an empirical environment which includes transparency (one of the three pillars of empiricism).

QUESTION 5

Steven is a Scrum Master that was hired to help an organization, that is new to Scrum, understands and enacts Scrum effectively. Which three activities would be acceptable? (Choose three.)

A. Require all teams in the organization to start using Scrum as soon as possible.
B. Arrange 1:1 coaching sessions to discuss any identified concerns Steven may have.
C. Schedule formal trainings.
D. Penalize any Scrum Team members who are not staying within the Scrum Framework.
E. Educate stakeholders and clients about Scrum.
F. Extend Retrospectives to include formal training.

Explanation:

The Scrum Master serves the organization in several ways, including: Leading and coaching the organization in its Scrum adoption; Planning Scrum implementations within the organization; Helping employees and stakeholders understand and enact Scrum and empirical product development.

QUESTION 6

A Scrum Team has been working on a product for several iterations and has an average velocity of 55 units of 'done' work per Sprint. A second team will be added to work on the same product.
What might be the impact on the original team?

A. Their velocity is likely not affected and will remain at 55.
B. Their velocity is likely to drop and be less than 55.
C. Their velocity is likely to rise and be more than 55.

Explanation:

Similar to membership changes within a single Scrum Team, adding or removing additional Scrum Teams working on the same product will impact productivity in the short term. Adding additional teams often go through recognizable stages as they change from being a collection of strangers to a united group with common goals. Bruce Tuckman's Forming, Storming, Norming, and Performing model describes these stages.

QUESTION 7

Which three statements best describe the purpose of having a Definition of Done? (Choose three.)

A. It is a checklist to monitor the Development Team member's progress on a task.
B. It provides guidance to the Development Team when they are forecasting their Sprint Backlog during the Sprint Planning.
C. As the Development Team is doing the work, it provides guidance on the remaining work needed to create the potentially shippable Increment by the end of the

Sprint.
D. It helps the Development Team defer any pending work to subsequent Sprints.
E. It creates transparency and provides a common understanding of the 'done' state of the Increment at the Sprint Review.
F. It helps the Scrum Team decide how much time is needed before the Sprint can end.

Explanation:

When a Product Backlog item or an Increment is described as 'Done', everyone must understand what 'Done' means. Scrum Team members must have a sharedunderstanding of what it means for work to be complete, to ensure transparency and is used to assess when work is complete on the product Increment. This Definition of Done provides the team guidance on what it takes to make the increment shippable.

QUESTION 8

Successful use of Scrum depends on how well people behave and act in ways that reflect the Scrum values. What can the value of openness affect?

A. Collaboration efforts.
B. Level of product quality.
C. Team member happiness.
D. Time to market.
E. Trust from stakeholders.
F. All of the above.

Explanation:

The Scrum Team and its stakeholders agree to be open about all the work and the challenges with performing the work.

QUESTION 9

What is management's role in Scrum?

A. To provide the necessary environment and support needed as defined by the Scrum Guide by providing insights and resources that help the Scrum Teams continue moving forward.
B. Identifying and removing people that are performing poorly.
C. Monitoring skill levels of the Development Team.
D. Monitoring the Development Team's velocity.

Explanation:

Getting the support from the business side helps facilitate the changes that fosters empiricism, self-organization, bottom-up intelligence, and intelligent release of software.

QUESTION 10

What would likely happen if management only changed the organization's current terminology to fit Scrum without the proper understanding and support of Scrum as defined in the Scrum Guide?

A. Very little change will happen as the vocabulary in Scrum is specifically defined for implementing Scrum.
B. The organization may not realize the real benefits of Scrum as there would be no real change on the way the teams work.
C. Organizations may feel less stressed as the behaviors would remain familiar to management.
D. All answers apply.

Explanation:

The defined terminology in Scrum was selected, designed, and defined specifically for supporting the Scrum Framework. Understanding the differences between traditional methods and the Scrum Framework will help move teams in the right direction in Scrum adoption.

QUESTION 11

Scrum is based on which of the following?

A. Defined process.
B. Complex process.
C. Empiricism.
D. Hybrid model

Explanation:

Scrum addresses complex problems in complex environments and asserts that knowledge comes from experience and making decisions based on what is known.What is known can only be discovered in hindsight.

QUESTION 12

Stakeholders are only allowed to meet with the Scrum Team at Sprint Review.

A. True
B. False

Explanation:

Getting feedback from Stakeholders is a crucial activity in Scrum. Working with stakeholders frequently ensures the team to focus on the right things to build. Although it is required to have Stakeholders at Sprint Review, they can also engage with the Scrum Team during Product Backlog Refinement, Sprint Planning or during the Sprint if the Scrum Team requires it.

QUESTION 13

Which Scrum Value is impacted by trust?

A. Respect
B. Courage
C. Commitment
D. Openness
E. Focus
F. All of the above

Explanation:

Without trust, team members will have difficulties acting and behaving in the ways that reflect the Scrum values and how effective they apply empiricism.

QUESTION 14

Doing your best and helping other Scrum Team members demonstrates which of the following?

A. Value of Commitment
B. Increased Revenue
C. Increased Profit
D. Maximizing utilization
E. High Performance

Explanation:

People personally commit to achieving the goals of the Scrum Team by doing their best and helping others.

QUESTION 15

Peter, a Project Manager, has raised concerns about your Scrum

Team's productivity and progress towards the objectives. Which is the

best way to respond to Peter's concerns?

A. Share the Product Backlog, the projections towards the release dates and ensure that Peter has access.
B. Show the Profit & Loss (P&L) report.
C. Share the current impediments.
D. Share the last stakeholder status report prepared by the Scrum Master.

Explanation:

One of the key pillars that support the empirical process control is Transparency. Transparency will help manage stakeholder expectations and allow the teams to effectively adapt if and when needed.

QUESTION 16

The three pillars of empirical process control consist of:

A. Planning, Inspection, Adaptation
B. Inspection, Transparency, Adaptation
C. Planning, Demonstration, Retrospective
D. Respect For People, Kaizen, Eliminating Waste

Explanation:

These three pillars uphold every implementation of the empirical process control. Without them, Scrum cannot be implemented as intended.

QUESTION 17

During Sprint Planning, the Definition of Done will help the Development Team forecast the amount of work, selected from the Product Backlog, deemed feasible to make 'done' by the end of the Sprint.

Which two items best describes what 'done' means? (Choose two.)

A. All the work needed to prepare the Increment for User Acceptance Testing.
B. All the work needed to prepare the Increment for Integration Testing.
C. Having an Increment of working software that is potentially releasable to the end users.
D. All the work performed as defined in the Definition of Done.
E. All the work completed within the current skills and expertise in the Development Team.

Explanation:

When a Product Backlog item or an Increment is described as 'Done', everyone must understand what 'Done' means. Although this may vary significantly per Scrum Team, members must have a shared understanding of what it means for work to be complete, to ensure transparency. This is the Definition of Done for theScrum Team and is used to assess when work is complete on the product Increment. The purpose of each Sprint is to deliver Increments of potentially releasable functionality that adhere to the Scrum Team's current Definition of Done.

QUESTION 18

Over the course of several Sprints, the relationship between the Product Owner and the Development team has suffered. The Development Team is upset with the Product Owner for the constantly changing the upcoming items for the product. The Product Owner is upset with the Development Team for changing the work that needs to be done during the Sprint.

What should Steven, the Scrum Master, do?

A. During the Sprint Retrospective, ask the Product Owner and the Development Team to address the issues. Have the Team discuss why the changes occur and what impact they have on the value of the product.
B. The Scrum Master's responsibility is to ensure the Development Team has a stable velocity. Any changes that negatively impact the team's velocity will be rejected by the Scrum Master.
C. Take the time between Sprints to organize a team building session to rebuild the relationship.
D. Explain to the Development Team that the Product Owner is accountable for flow of value and needs to be followed in order to maximize the value delivered.

Explanation:

Conflicts are a natural occurrence and the Scrum Master coaches the Development Team on the value of resolving conflicts. Leaving conflicts unresolved can impact the Scrum values of openness and respect diminishing trust. Lower trust levels will impact the Scrum Team's effectiveness and can cause impediments inthe future. It is the responsibility of the Scrum Master to remove impediments that hinder the team through conflict resolution and facilitation.

QUESTION 19

You have been hired as a Scrum Master for a company that has been doing business for over fifty years. In order to stay competitive, they have started an initiative to digitize their legacy systems. The company has several Scrum Teams working on different components that will be integrated to a single back office platform.

Your team is responsible for building the back office platform and integrating all other components. The Scrum Teams work in two week Sprints and are expected todeliver all functionality in six Sprints.

During development the requirement changes in the other components have been slowing down your team's progress. Because of these changes, your team has estimated that they will not be able to deliver all expected work within the original timeframe. The Scrum Teams working on the other components confirm that they are still on track to meet the expected delivery date. The program manager in charge of the digitization initiative is upset and angry with your team.

As a Scrum Master, what could you do to help the Product Owner?

A. You suggest working with the program manager and the other teams on the ordering and the value of your team's open Product Backlog items to redefine the possible delivery date.
B. You shorten your team's Sprints to be ready sooner.
C. You remove all items from the Product Backlog for which development is forecasted to be beyond the expected date. These are likely to be low value anyhow.
D. You suggest adding additional developers to the team in order to increase velocity and meet the original date.

Explanation:

The Scrum Master serves the Product Owner in several ways, including:
- Finding techniques for effective Product Backlog management;
- Helping the Scrum Team understand the need for clear and concise
- Product Backlog items;Understanding product planning in an empirical environment;
- Ensuring the Product Owner knows how to arrange the Product Backlog to maximize value.

QUESTION 20

Steven is a Scrum Master for three different teams building a single product from the same Product Backlog. Development Team members from each team haveapproached Steven complaining that their teams need Nicole, an external specialist, to commit full time for their next Sprint.

Which three acceptable solutions would Steven consider? (Choose three.)

A. For Sprints that require Nicole's expertise for more than one team, combine the teams into one and separate when they no longer need to share her services.
B. Investigate whether applying additional techniques or frameworks for scaling Scrum would be appropriate for this product team in the future, since you have multiple Scrum Teams working on the same product, with dependencies between the teams.
C. People from the Development Teams with an interest in Nicole's domain could volunteer to take on this work in their respective teams.
D. Ask Nicole for a plan to hire and train additional people in her domain, and in the meantime work with the Product Owner and Development Teams to re-prioritize the work so that tasks not depending on Nicole can be done first.
E. Have the Development Team re-order the Product Backlog so Nicole can serve one team full-time in a Sprint.
F. Create a team with Nicole and people from the teams to temporarily work in Nicole's domain to serve the existing teams.

Explanation:

The Scrum Master is responsible for removing impediments within the current context of the situation AND boundaries defined by the Scrum framework.

QUESTION 21
Which two scenarios would best represent a self-organizing
Development Team? (Choose two.)
A. The Development Team members are strictly focused on the work
   within their functional role and always handing off the work to other
   roles in a timely matter.
B. Management works with the Scrum Master to optimize the
   Development Team's progress during the Sprint.
C. Development Team members collaboratively select and re-plan their
   work throughout the Sprint.
D. The Development Team invites external people to the Sprint Planning
   to help them create a complete and detailed Sprint Backlog.
E. The Development Team creates its own Sprint Backlog, reflecting all
   work that is part of the Definition of Done.

Explanation:
A self-organized team is a team that is able to self-manage and decide
how best to accomplish their work.

QUESTION 22
Steven is a Scrum Master of a Development Team that has members
working in different cities and time zones. Organizing the Scrum events
is time consumingand requires a lot of effort to set up and run. The
Development Team proposes to only hold the Daily Scrum on Mondays.

Which two responses would be most appropriate from Steven? (Choose
two.)
A. Coach the team on why having a Daily Scrum every day is an
   important opportunity to update the Sprint plan and how it helps the
   team self-organize work toward achieving the Sprint Goal.
B. Ensure that there is an overall consensus by having the Development
   Team members vote.
C. Help the Development Team understand that lowering the frequency
   of communication will only increase the feeling of disconnect between
   the team members.
D. Acknowledge and support their decision.

Explanation:
The Scrum Master is responsible for ensuring that the Scrum Team
understands the purpose and value of the Scrum events. Because the
Daily Scrum is owned bythe Development Team, it will decide how best
to run the event. And if needed the Scrum Master will coach the team to
ensure the decisions stay within the boundaries of the Scrum
framework.

QUESTION 23

Steven is a Scrum Master of a Scrum Team that is new to Scrum. At the halfway point of the Sprint, the Product Owner comes to Steven telling him that he isconcerned the Development Team will not be able to complete the entire Sprint Backlog by the end of the Sprint.

What should Steven do in this situation?

A. Motivate the Development Team to meet their commitment to the Product Owner.
B. Coach the Product Owner that with complex software development, you cannot promise the entire scope that was forecast during Sprint Planning. As more is learned during the Sprint, work may emerge that affects the Sprint Backlog.
C. Advise the Product Owner that the Development Team owns the Sprint Backlog and it is up to them to meet their commitments. No one tells the DevelopmentTeam how to turn Product Backlog into Increments of potentially releasable functionality.
D. Add more people to the Development Team to meet the Product Owner's expectations.

Explanation:

Scrum is founded on empirical process control theory, or empiricism. Empiricism asserts that knowledge comes from experience and making decisions based on what is known. The Sprint Backlog is a forecast by the Development Team about what functionality will be in the next Increment and the work needed to deliver that functionality into a 'Done' Increment. The Development Team modifies the Sprint Backlog throughout the Sprint, and the Sprint Backlog emerges during the Sprint. This emergence occurs as the Development Team works through the plan and learns more about the work needed to achieve the Sprint Goal.

Why C is incorrect:
a) The Dev Team does not commit to finishing all items in the Sprint Backlog. Committing to completing all items would be fixed scope and fixed time leaving no room to adapt. They commit to the Sprint Goal and doing the right thing.
b) It's also incorrect for the PO to focus on completing the entire Sprint Backlog. Finishing everything should not be his main focus. Having a shippable increment that meets the Sprint Goal is more important than trying to finish everything. The advice in option C is equivalent to "Don't worry, they'll get everything done." butbecause of the complex domain, you cannot guarantee everything will get done.

QUESTION 24

During the Sprint Review, the Product Owner decides to release the current Increment to production. The stakeholders suggest temporarily delaying the next Sprint in order to respond more quickly to user feedback after the release. The Product Owner prefers to continue to the next Sprint and make progress towards the next release. Steven, the Scrum Master, begins facilitating the discussion.

What would be two acceptable outcomes of the discussion? (Choose two.)

A. Continue with the Sprints and include the customer feedback in the Product Backlog.
B. Delay the next Sprint to allow the Development Team to work on new customer feedback.
C. Continue with the Sprints but shorten the Sprint time-boxes to allow for shorter feedback loops.
D. Continue with the Sprints but allow the Sprint Goal within the Sprint to change according to the customer feedback.

Explanation:

A new Sprint starts immediately after the conclusion of the previous Sprint. Delaying the start of the next Sprint interrupts progress and can reduce the Time-to- Market. Shortening the Sprint length allows the team to respond quicker to changes outside of the Sprint plan and while still allowing delivery of business value. Adding user feedback to the Product Backlog helps the Product Owner with ordering the backlog to maximize the flow of value.

During the Sprint no changes are made that would endanger the Sprint Goal.

QUESTION 25

At the Sprint Planning, the Development Team is not able to forecast the number of Product Backlog items it can do in the upcoming Sprint due to unclear requirements. The Product Owner, however, was able to clearly define the business objective he hopes to achieve in the Sprint.

Which of the following two actions would you support? (Choose two.)

A. The Development Team forecasts the most likely Product Backlog items to meet the business objective and create a Sprint Backlog based on a likely initial design and plan. Once the time- box for the Sprint Planning meeting is over, they start implementation and continue to analyze, decompose, and create additional functionality during the Sprint.
B. If all agree they can extend the Sprint Planning until the Development Team can forecast enough Product Backlog items before starting the implementation.
C. Allow the Development Team members as much time as needed to review the Product Backlog items and reconvene with the Product Owner when they are confident enough to make a forecast for the Sprint.
D. They discuss in the upcoming Sprint Retrospective why this happened and what changes will make it less likely to occur again.

Explanation:

All events are time-boxed events, such that every event has a maximum duration. The Development Team modifies the Sprint Backlog throughout the Sprint, and the Sprint Backlog emerges during the Sprint. This emergence occurs as the Development Team works through the plan and learns more about the work needed toachieve the Sprint Goal.

QUESTION 26

Steven is a Scrum Master on a new Scrum Team.
What would be the best way for him to determine if the Product Owner is interacting enough with the Development Team during a Sprint?

A. Check whether the Product Owner is actively engaged at the Daily Scrums.

B. Check whether the Increment presented at the Sprint Review meets the Product Owner's expectations.

C. See whether the Product Owner has provided enough information at the Sprint Planning to make his/her presence optional during the Sprint. The level of autonomy within Development Team can be the result of having the right presence from the Product Owner.

D. The Product Owner must always be present with the Development Team. Unavailability of the Product Owner is prohibited in Scrum.

Explanation:
Outcomes of the Scrum Team are affected by the Product Owner's participation and availability. During a Sprint he/she is responsible for answering questions from the Development Team about items in the current Sprint and optimizing the value of the work the Development Team does.

QUESTION 27

In what two ways is velocity and technical debt related? (Choose two.)
A. They are not related because technical debt is non-functional and velocity is calculated based on end user functionality.

B. As the Development Team is working on new Product Backlog items, they may unexpectedly run into technical debt that will result the team's velocity dropping.

C. A Development Team can artificially increase velocity by allowing technical debt to be incurred.

D. Adding estimates to technical debt will allow the Development Team to maintain constant velocity therefore ensuring predictability.

Explanation:

Technical debt is a natural occurrence when developing complex products. It is a concept in software development that reflects the implied cost of additional rework caused by choosing an easy solution now instead of using a better approach that would take longer. And how it is managed will depend on the team AND context of the situation.

QUESTION 28

If burndown charts are used to visualize progress, what does a trendline through a release burndown chart indicate?

A. When all work will be completed so the Scrum Team can start work on a new Product Backlog.
B. When the project will be over if the Product Owner removes work that is equal in effort to any new work that is added.
C. When the work remaining is projected to be completed if nothing changes on the Product Backlog or Development Team.
D. The evolution of the return of investment on the project.

Explanation:

The trendline is based on the team's average velocity and the projective completion to zero is based on the team's velocity. The burndown chart is a helpful tool for Development Teams to self-manage BUT it is not mandatory as the teams will decide the best way to manage their own progress and promote transparency.

QUESTION 29

What is a good way for a Scrum Team to ensure that security concerns are addressed and transparent?

A. Add Security Sprints to resolve security concerns when needed.
B. Have the Scrum Team create Product Backlog items for each concern and/or add security concerns to the definition of "Done".
C. Create a separate backlog for security items and only work on the items when a specialist becomes available.
D. Delegate the work to an external team.

Explanation:

The Product Backlog and the Definition of "Done" are artifacts that promote transparency.

QUESTION 30

Technical Debt can lead to false assumptions about the current state of the system and the Increment reviewed at the end of the Sprint.

A. True
B. False

Explanation:

Technical debt is any shortcomings in the code. It is a natural by-product of software development (unavoidable) and can at best be managed. If neglected, it will compound and have a negative effect on the team's ability to the deliver value. A team can have an artificially high velocity by taking shortcuts or introducing technical, debt into the system. This can give a false assumption about the current state of the product. It can look good on the surface but underneath can be a mess.

QUESTION 31

Select the correct Scrum Team roles defined in Scrum.

A. Development Team, Scrum Master, Product Owner
B. Engineers, Business Analyst, Product Owner
C. Stakeholders, Scrum Master, Project Manager, Product Owner
D. Product Manager, Business Analyst, Development Team, Stakeholders

Explanation:

The Scrum Framework only recognizes these three roles although others may be needed to help the team build the most valuable product possible.

QUESTION 32

Scrum has a role called "Project Manager."

A. True
B. False

Explanation:

The Scrum Framework only recognizes three roles although others may be needed to help the team build the most valuable product possible.

QUESTION 33

A Scrum Team has been working on the same product for twelve Sprints. What would likely be the immediate impact on the original Scrum Team if two new ScrumTeams are to be added the same product?

A. Its productivity is likely to decrease.
B. Its productivity is likely to increase.
C. Its productivity is likely to stay the same.

Explanation:

The productivity of the original Scrum Team would likely decrease as they would need to take time to assist and support the new Scrum Teams in order for them to perform optimally.

QUESTION 34

A Scrum Team must have a Product Owner and Scrum Master.

A. False. A Scrum Master is only necessary when requested or needed.
B. True. Each must be a full-time member on the Scrum Team.
C. True. Their participation and availability will impact the outcomes produced by the Scrum Team.
D. False. If a Product Owner is unavailable, he/she can be replaced by a Business Analyst.

Explanation:

A Product Owner or Scrum Master can be dedicated to one team OR participate as a member on more than one team. How much time they spend with each teamwill directly impact effectiveness of the team.

QUESTION 35

A new member has just joined an existing Development Team that has been together for several Sprints. During the Sprint, the individual has been trying to share his ideas and viewpoints but is continuously ignored by the rest of the Development Team.

Which three Scrum Values has the Development Team been neglecting? (Choose three.)

A. Commitment
B. Respect
C. Transparency
D. Focus
E. Openness
F. Courage

Explanation

The Scrum Team members have courage to do the right thing and work on challenging problems. The Scrum Team agree to be open (to speak and listen) about allthe work and the challenges with performing the work. Scrum Team members respect each other's skills, experience, and opinions.

QUESTION 36
Which two behaviors would reflect Servant Leadership in a Scrum Master? (Choose two.)

A. Facilitating Scrum Events as requested or needed.
B. Coaching the Development Team, the Product Owner and the organization on how to work empirically.
C. Staying away from internal Development Team interactions, maximizing their autonomy and freedom.
D. Resolving every impediment for the Development Team.

Explanation:
The Scrum Master is responsible for serving the team by facilitating and removing impediments to ensure there are minimal roadblocks in the way of the team. The Scrum Master also coaches the Scrum Team and organization to ensure the benefits of Scrum is realized.

"Removing every impediment for the Development Team" may seem like the right thing to do but by doing it this way, the Dev Team's ability to self-organize would be limited. There are some impediments that will depend solely on the Scrum Master and there will be some that require collaboration with the Dev Team. The former might be working with the finance department to renew services that the team is using. The latter might be lack of skills to make a particular item done. TheScrum Master can coach the team on finding different solutions to resolve the issue.

"Removing impediments" is good. "Removing **every** impediment **for the Development Team**" is not so good and sometimes not even possible.

QUESTION 37

Collaboration issues and technical dependencies between multiple Scrum Teams working on the same product can be fully resolved by using the correct version control tools.

A. True
B. False

Explanation
When working on complex problems in complex environments, it cannot be guaranteed that applying a specific process or tool will fix the problem. Although, process and tools are important it's more important that people collaborate and try to find different solutions together and not rely solely on a tool to fix the problem.

QUESTION 38

You have a Scrum Team that has been working together for over a year. The Development Team consists of eleven members who rarely collaborate and work within their functional boundaries. There are no Sprint Goals and most of the items in the Sprint Backlog are unrelated. The Scrum Team has concluded that it is not possible to create Sprint Goals based on the items in the Product Backlog.

What might explain why the Scrum Team is finding it difficult to craft Sprint Goals? (Choose all that apply.)

A. The Sprints are too long.
B. The Product Owner is not empowered to make decisions about items in the Product Backlog nor how they are ordered.
C. The Product Owner doesn't set objectives that he/she wants to achieve with upcoming Sprints.
D. Scrum might not be the best framework for this team.
E. The Development Team is too big.

Explanation:

Many people misinterpret the Scrum Guide as stating the Development Team size is limited to 3-9 members. In reality, it only states that there is inherent risk attached to having less than 3 members and more than 9 members. As the number of members increases, the lines of communication also increase. This can be calculated using the Group intercommunication formula: $n(n - 1) / 2$ where n is the number of members. Some teams are able to handle the risk and "synergize" whereas others might struggle. Saying that, the relationship between defining a Sprint Goal and Development Team size is unclear.

But the relationship between the ordering of the Product Backlog, the PO having clear objectives, and the Sprint Goal are *direct*. The Product Owner typically comes to the Sprint Planning with a business objective in mind and Product Backlog items related to the business objective. After deciding what can be done for the upcoming Sprint, the Scrum Team will craft a Sprint Goal that would be met through the implementation of the items. This is not dependent on the size of the team nor length of the Sprint.

Scrum is also a framework that's fit for purpose. Some projects/products are not fit for Scrum... or, better stated, Scrum is not suitable for all projects/products.

QUESTION 39

According to the Scrum Guide, where should the Daily Scrum be held?

A. Wherever the Development Team decides is most suitable.
B. In a room where management can attend.
C. In the same location where the Development Team is seated.
D. In front of the Scrum board.
E. Wherever the Scrum Master decides is best.

Explanation:

Because the Daily Scrum is owned and managed by the Development Team, it is up to them to decide on the most effective place and time to hold the Daily Scrum.

QUESTION 40

Adding more resources in Scrum will proportionally increase the value delivered.

A. True
B. False

Explanation:

When working on complex problems in complex environments, adding more resources (people, money, tools, etc.) cannot guarantee increased value or success.

QUESTION 41

Steven, who is a Scrum Master, on one of the Scrum Teams has approached you asking for advice. Their Daily Scrum requires more than 15 minutes and the teamhas suggested dividing themselves into two separate teams in order to stay within the time box.

As another Scrum Master, what would be the best response?

A. Agree - this is an appropriate solution to the problem.

B. Disagree - as the root cause may not be that the team is too big.

C. Unsure - dividing a team into two cannot be decided based on this information. You offer to observe.

D. Agree – You agree that dividing the team into two is a good strategy to allow the teams to learn how to run Daily Scrums quickly and effectively. Once they've learned to limit the Daily Scrum to 15 minutes, you can merge the teams again.

Explanation:

The relationship between cause and effect can become more clear when more information emerges.

QUESTION 42

An organization is using Scrum to build five new products.
What would be the best two options for the number of Product Owners the organization should have? (Choose two.)

A. There is one Product Owner for each product (so five in total). Each Product Owner may delegate, share and align work within their individual Product Backlog.

B. Enough Product Owners to delegate as much work needed to maximize utilization of all Development Team members.

C. There is one Product Owner responsible for all five products. This person is not allowed to delegate any of the Product Owner responsibilities as he/she is accountable for the success of each product.

D. There is one Product Owner responsible for all five products. In order to scale his/her role, he/she can delegate some of the individual Product Owner responsibilities to others within each product but would still remain accountable for the value of the work produced.

Explanation:

The Product Owner is the sole person responsible for maximizing the value of the product through the ordering and management of the Product Backlog. This reduces complexity in communication and understanding who to go to when there are questions about the product. The Product Owner may delegate his/her responsibilities but still remains accountable for the outcome of those responsibilities.

QUESTION 43

During the Sprint Review of a scaled development effort, each Scrum Team should demonstrate its individual Increment in a separate branch of the code.

A. True
B. False

Explanation:

If there are multiple Scrum Teams working on the system or product release, the Development Teams on all the Scrum Teams must mutually define the definition of"Done". Each Increment is additive to all prior Increments and thoroughly tested, ensuring that all Increments work together.

QUESTION 44

The director of engineering in your organization always stresses the importance of meeting deadlines in order for the engineering department to be seen as a reliable source for the product management department. The director has calculated that the team's velocity needs to increase an additional 15% to meet the commitment he made to management for the release date of the product.

He asks Steven, the team's Scrum Master, to increase his team's velocity. Which would be the best two responses for Steven to take? (Choose two.)

A. He explains how a team uses the velocity of a Sprint primarily to forecast work for the next Sprint, not to perfectly predict future productivity. He refers the director to the Product Owner for all information concerning the progress of development.
B. He informs the director of organizational impediments he is aware of that prevent the team from being more productive. He suggests collaborating with him on how to remove these impediments.
C. He educates his director how it is part of a team's self-organization to improve velocity. He invites the director to the next Sprint Retrospective to brainstorm on how they can improve.
D. He helps the director understand that it typically takes a few Sprints for a team to gradually increase the velocity up to the level expected. Meanwhile he presents this to the team as a challenge and a company goal, leaving it however up to them to figure out exactly how to achieve this.
E. He tells the director that this is not his responsibility in Scrum. He tells the director to work with the Product Owner to check whether the estimates on the Product Backlog are being respected during implementation.

Explanation:

The Scrum Master serves the organization by helping employees and stakeholders understand and enact Scrum and empirical product development and causing change that increases the productivity of the Scrum Team.

QUESTION 45

In what ways does the Scrum Master keep a Development Team working at its highest level of productivity?

A. By removing impediments that hinder the Development Team and facilitating Development Team decisions.
B. By helping the Development Team with user acceptance tests and tracking defects.
C. By ensuring each member takes turns speaking at the Daily Scrum and ending the event on time.
D. By keeping the Scrum board and burn-down chart updated daily.

Explanation:

The Scrum Master serves the Development Team by removing impediments to the Development Team's progress and facilitating Scrum events as requested orneeded.

QUESTION 46

Which of the following statements are true about the Scrum Master role?

A. The Scrum Master assigns the tasks to Development Team members and ensures they are completed within the committed timebox.
B. The Scrum Master helps those outside the Scrum Team understand which interactions are helpful and teaches the Development Team to keep the Scrummeetings within the timebox.
C. The Scrum Master is responsible for updating the Scrum board and ensuring team members avoid conflicts.
D. At the Sprint Review, the Scrum Master demonstrates the completed Increment and answers any questions from the stakeholders.

Explanation:

The Scrum Master is responsible not only for coaching the Scrum Team but also the organization.

QUESTION 47

Your organization has formed a new Scrum Team and has assigned you as the Scrum Master.In what ways would you help the team start?

A. Ensure the Scrum Team members have compatible personalities, have the tech leads clarify the expectations and responsibilities of each role, and propose a performance rewards system.
B. Have the Scrum Team members introduce their background experience with each other, ask the Product Owner to discuss the product and answer questions,and ensure the team understands the need for a Definition of "Done."

Explanation:

Scrum Teams should have all of the competencies and skills to do the work in the Product Backlog which includes understanding the goals and history of the product and ensuring that they all know what "done" means.

QUESTION 48

What action can the Scrum Master take to ensure communication between the Development Team and Product Owner is effective?

A. Ensure all communication goes through the Scrum Master first.
B. Teach the Product Owner to talk in terms of technology and technical requirements.
C. Observe the communications between them and facilitate discussions if needed or by request.
D. Translate the technologies used by the Development Team in order for the Product Owner to make decisions.

Explanation:

One of the primary responsibilities of a Scrum Master is the ability to facilitate regardless of the context or setting.

QUESTION 49

Which statement is FALSE in regards to the Sprint Goal?

A. It is only a forecast and changes during the Sprint as more is learned.

B. If it doesn't seem achievable, the Development Team has the courage to tell the Product Owner.

C. The Product Owner respects the Development Team's opinion on whether they can achieve it.

D. It helps increase focus.

E. The Scrum Team discusses openly about alternative ways to reach it.

F. The Development Team commits to it.

Explanation:

The Sprint Goal is an objective set for the Sprint that can be met through the implementation of Product Backlog. It provides guidance to the Development Team on why it is building the Increment.

QUESTION 50

During a Product Backlog refinement meeting, the Product Owner introduces a business objective that will be worked on for the next several Sprints. The ProductOwner envisions several key features necessary to be delivered in order to meet the business objective. As the features will be using sensitive user data it will be subjected to external security audits. These non-functional security requirements were not applicable to previous Increments.
What are two good ways the Development Team can handle these high-security concerns? (Choose two.)

A. They should be planned in parallel Sprints so not to disrupt the Development Team during feature development. After security concerns have been finalized, they will be applied to the work that is already completed before new feature development can continue.

B. They should be handled in a parallel Sprint by a separate security team so that security can be resolved through application enhancements without impacting the functional development.

C. A complete list of security-related Product Backlog items needs to be created before starting a new Sprint.

D. During the Sprint Retrospective, the Development Team assesses how to add these expectations to their Definition of Done so every future Increment will meet these security requirements. If needed they can work with external specialists to better understand the requirements.

E. They are added to the Product Backlog and addressed throughout the next Sprints, combined with creating the business functionality in those Sprints, no matter how small the business functionality.

Explanation:

In order to ensure transparency, work that must be done to the product must be visible in either the Product Backlog or the Definition of Done.

QUESTION 51

How should a Scrum Master coordinate the work when more than one Scrum Team is working on one product?

A. Teach them that it's their responsibility to coordinate with the other teams to integrate and create a shippable product Increment at the end of every Sprint.
B. Identify and manage the dependencies between Scrum Teams.
C. Have the Product Owner work with the tech leads of each team to parse the Product Backlog and minimize overlap in User Stories.
D. Merge the teams and work from a single Sprint Backlog.

Explanation:

One of the benefits of self-organized teams is the ability to decide how best to work together to produce a shippable Increment.

QUESTION 52

What would be typical Scrum Master activities during the Sprint?

A. Monitor the progress of the Development Team and assigning tasks.
B. Remove impediments and facilitating inspection and adaptation opportunities as requested or needed.
C. Avoiding conflicts and escalating to the line managers if conflicts occur.

QUESTION 53

A Scrum Master teaches those who are interested in the Development Team's progress that progress in Scrum comes from inspecting an Increment at the SprintReview.

A. True
B. False

Explanation:

Working software is the primary measure of progress.

QUESTION 54

As a Scrum Master, what would you strive for if five new Scrum Teams were to work on one product?

A. There should be five Product Owners, one for each Scrum Team.
B. The product has one Product Backlog and one Product Owner.
C. There should be five Product Backlogs and one Product Owner to manage them.
D. There should be five Product Backlogs and five Product Owners.

Explanation:

For a single product there is one Product Backlog. For a single Product Backlog there is one Product Owner.

QUESTION 55

Several Sprints into a project, a client is complaining to the Product

Owner about the poor performance of the product. As a Scrum Master,

how can you help the Product Owner?

A. Coach the Product Owner on effective ways to communicate this concern to the Development Team and encourage the Product Owner to add the performanceissue to the Product Backlog.

B. Tell the Product Owner performance is defined by the Development Team.

C. Note the issue for the next Sprint Retrospective.

D. Notify the team responsible for system performance.

QUESTION 56

How should a Scrum Master divide a group of 100 people into multiple Development Teams?

A. Create teams based on their functional layer.
B. Have the resource manager assign the people to teams.
C. Ask the developers to divide themselves into teams.

Explanation:

A good first question for you to suggest the group thinking about when forming into teams is "How will we make sure all teams have the right amount of expertise?"

QUESTION 57

You are the Scrum Master for four Scrum Teams working on one product. Several of the developers notify you that their teams will need full-time help of an external technical specialist in the upcoming two Sprints.

What key concerns should the Scrum Master take into account?

A. Having enough work for all Development Team members.
B. The benefit of Development Teams solving the problem themselves and the ability to produce integrated Increments.
C. Maintaining a consistent velocity.
D. Hiring additional resources to fill the void in skillset.

QUESTION 58

Which of the following is true about the Product Owner role?

A. Can be shared between multiple people on a Scrum Team, Is the same as a Project Manager. Is played by a committee or a team of people.
B. Is one person. Can be influenced by a committee. Is accountable for ordering the Product Backlog.

QUESTION 59

Which role is responsible for engaging with stakeholders?

A. The team lead
B. The business analyst
C. The project manager
D. The Development Team
E. The Product Owner

QUESTION 60

Which stakeholder is the most important for the Product Owner to satisfy?

A. The company founder
B. The board of directors
C. The Head of Product
D. The Product's users

Explanation:

The highest priority is to satisfy the end users.

QUESTION 61

Customer satisfaction should be measured:

A. Annually
B. Quarterly
C. Daily
D. Frequently

Explanation:

Frequent enough to ensure the team is building the right thing at the right time but not so frequent it hinders the team from the work.

QUESTION 62

Why is it important that there is only one Product Owner per product?

A. The Scrum Master knows who will be his back-up whenever he is unavailable, it saves the organization time and money, and the Development Team knows who to request tasks from.
B. It is clear who is accountable for the ultimate success of the product, the Development Team always knows who determines priorities, and it helps avoid barriers to effective communication and rapid decision-making.
C. It isn't important as multiple Product Owners can easily share a single Product Backlog.

QUESTION 63

Which of these tools is mandatory for the Product Owner to use?

A. Release burnup chart.
B. Burndown chart.
C. Version control.
D. Project Gantt chart.
E. None of the above.

Explanation:

The Product Owner can use any tool, method or practice that he/she finds fit in order for him/her to make the best decisions possible.

QUESTION 64

Who is responsible for ensuring the Product Backlog items are understood to the level needed?

A. The Business Analyst.
B. The Scrum Master.
C. The Development Team.
D. The Product Owner.

Explanation:
The Product Owner is accountable for managing the Product Backlog.

QUESTION 65

What activities would a Product Owner do during an active Sprint?

A. Engage with the stakeholders and answer questions from the Development Team.
B. Prioritize the Sprint Backlog.
C. Participate at the Daily Scrum.
D. Update the burndown chart.

QUESTION 66

Who manages the progress of work during a Sprint?

A. The Scrum Master
B. The Product Owner
C. The Team Lead
D. The Development Team

Explanation:

The Development Team is self-organized, thus manages and decides how to manage their own progress.

QUESTION 67

What should the Development Team do if they are approached by someone outside the team and asked to add a "very important" item to a Sprint that is in

progress?

A. Add the item to the bottom of the Sprint Backlog.
B. Replace an item in the current Sprint of equal size.
C. Add the item to the top of the next Sprint Backlog.
D. Inform the Product Owner so he/she can work with the person.

Explanation:

Allow the Product Owner to decide what to do with the item as he/she is responsible for the flow of value.

QUESTION 68

The Development Team should have all the skills and competencies needed to:

A. Turn the Product Backlog items it selects into a potentially releasable product increment of functionality.
B. Do all of the development work in order to handoff to the testers in the subsequent Sprint.
C. Complete the project within the estimate as committed to the Product Owner.

QUESTION 69

How often should Development Team membership change?

A. Frequently in order to share knowledge.
B. As needed, while taking into account a short term reduction in productivity.
C. Never, as it conflicts with the Scrum process.
D. As needed, as long as it doesn't impact productivity.

Explanation:

It is not mandatory that the same team stay together, although it must be understood that any changes to the team will impact how they work together.

QUESTION 70

What is the Development Team responsible for?

A. Writing User Stories and ordering the Product Backlog.
B. Reporting productivity and selecting the Sprint time-box.
C. Organizing the work required to meet the Sprint Goal and resolving internal team conflicts.

QUESTION 71

According to Scrum theory, how should a group of fifty people be divided into multiple Development Teams?

A. Allow the team leads to divide and select teams.
B. Understanding the product, the product vision and the Scrum framework, the group self-organizes into teams.
C. Create a skills matrix, identify role levels, and years of experience to assign people to teams.
D. The teams will rotate members every Sprint to spread knowledge.

QUESTION 72

What is the recommended size for a Development Team (within the Scrum Team)?

A. 3 to 9
B. Minimal 5
C. 7 plus or minus 2
D. 9

QUESTION 73

What should a Development Team do if they don't understand a functional requirement?

A. Request a specialist to be added to the Development Team.
B. Move the item to a future Sprint.
C. Complete as much as possible and add the remaining work as a new Product Backlog item.
D. Work with the Product Owner to determine what is possible and acceptable.

QUESTION 74

What should a Development Team do if it realizes it has selected too much work after starting the Sprint?

A. Modify the definition of "Done" to ensure all Product Backlog items can be done by the end of the Sprint.
B. Work with the Product Owner to remove some work or Product Backlog items as soon as possible.
C. Add additional team members to handle the extra work.
D. Continue working and update the Product Owner at the Sprint Review.

Explanation:

The Sprint Backlog is a living artifact that evolves and changes as more is learned or discovered.

QUESTION 75

What would be the responsibilities of a self-organizing Development Team?

A. Update stakeholders on the daily progress and keep the burn-down chart updated.
B. Select the Product Backlog items for the Sprint and do the work planned in the Sprint Backlog.
C. Writing User Stories and reordering the Product Backlog.
D. Deciding on the value of the product features and value estimations.

QUESTION 76

How should multiple Scrum Teams, working from the same Product Backlog, select the Product Backlog items their teams plan to work on?

A. The Product Owner will present the work and the Development Teams will select the items they will work on.
B. The Product Owner creates separate Product Backlogs for each Development Team.
C. Each Scrum Team would select an equal number of items.
D. The Product Owner assigns the work to each team.
E. The Scrum Team with the highest productivity will select the items first.

Explanation:

The ones doing the work are the best ones to decide what they can do and how to do it.

QUESTION 77

What would be good ways of creating Development Teams that would support the Scrum values?

A. Project Managers will allocate individuals to specific teams.
B. Bring all the developers or existing teams together and let them propose how to organize into the new structure and self-organize into Development Teams.
C. The operations manager determines the new team structures and assignments.
D. Direct managers personally re-assign current reports to new teams.

Explanation:

The ones that will be doing the work are the best ones to decide on what Development Team structures work best.

QUESTION 78

Which role is responsible for determining when it is most appropriate to update the Sprint Backlog?

A. The Product Owner
B. The Development Team
C. The Scrum Team
D. The Scrum Master

Explanation:

The Development Team is responsible for tracking the remaining work of the Sprint.

QUESTION 79

Part of the team's Definition of "Done" requires creating or updating technical documentation in order to maintain the product and/or features in the future. The team's technical writer will be on vacation during the Sprint.

What should you do?

A. Encourage the technical writers from other teams to form a specialized team to organize and plan the work for multiple teams.
B. The Development Team members will write it as they are still responsible for creating the documentation to make the Increment done in conformance with their Definition of "Done."
C. Wait until the technical writer returns before continuing with related items.
D. Complete all development work first while adding technical documentation to the Product Backlog to be done in a subsequent Sprint.

Explanation:

All Product Backlog items selected for the Sprint are owned by the Development Team as a whole. Although individual members may work on specific tasks, the Development Team is still accountable for doing the work to deliver a shippable Increment.

QUESTION 80

Kevin is a senior developer that has recently joined an existing Scrum Team. The existing team members are unable to get along with Kevin and conclude that he is not a culture fit.

If necessary, who is responsible for removing the new team member, and why?

A. The Scrum Master because he/she is responsible for removing Impediments.
B. The Development Team is responsible because it is an internal team issue, and may request help from the Scrum Master.
C. The HR department, as they are responsible for the hiring process.
D. The Product Owner because he/she is responsible for managing the team.

Explanation:

The ones closest to the problem are the best ones to understand and solve the problems. The Scrum Master can remove members (if empowered). The question is focused on the ownership of the root problem. The Development Team is responsible for addressing internal conflicts and may request help from the Scrum Master if needed. Because this is a localized issue, they are the ones that must initiate the actions for the results they desire.

QUESTION 81

A cross-functional Development Team is defined as:

A. Cross-skilled individuals who are able to do all the work necessary to deliver a shippable Increment at the end of the Sprint.
B. A team of engineers, testers, business analysts, technical architects and functional managers.
C. A group of full-stack developers shared across multiple teams.
D. A team of skilled developers that can effectively multi-task on multiple Product Backlog items at the same time.

Explanation:

The objective of the Sprint is to produce a shippable Increment at the end of each Sprint so that the team can effectively inspect and adapt accordingly.

QUESTION 82

Who must ensure that the work done for a Product Backlog item conforms to the Definition of "Done?"

A. The test team.
B. The Scrum Team.
C. The Scrum Master.
D. The Product Owner.
E. The Development Team.

Explanation:

The Development Team owns the Definition of "Done" and is accountable for the quality of the Product Backlog items.

QUESTION 83

The Scrum Master is no longer needed when teams become self-organized.

A. True
B. False

QUESTION 84

What Product Owner activities occur between the end of the current Sprint and the beginning of the next Sprint?

A. Product Backlog refinement.
B. Updating stakeholders on project progress.
C. There are no such activities. When the current Sprint ends, the new Sprint begins.
D. Participate as a team member at the Sprint Retrospective.

QUESTION 85

What factors are best considered when defining the Sprint length?

A. How often team membership changes and the size of the Development Team.
B. Having consistent Sprint length across all Scrum Teams.
C. The level of expertise over the technology to be used, ability to release an Increment to the end users, and the risk of being disconnected from the stakeholders.

QUESTION 86

Which of the following are feedback loops in Scrum?

A. Daily Scrum, Sprint Review, and Sprint Retrospective
B. Daily Standup, Sprint Review, and Sprint Retrospective
C. Release Planning, Daily Scrum, and Sprint Review
D. Grooming, Daily Status, and Sprint Review

QUESTION 87

What could be a reason for a Product Owner to delay the start of a new Sprint after the conclusion of the previous Sprint?

A. The QA team has not finished testing the previous Increment before declaring it ready to ship.
B. The stakeholders were disappointed with the Increment produced in the previous Sprint.
C. There is no acceptable reason. A new Sprint starts immediately after the conclusion of the previous Sprint.
D. The Product Owner needs additional time to identify the next initiatives.
E. There's not enough work in the Product Backlog to work on in the upcoming Sprint.

QUESTION 88

Which of the following is required in Scrum?

A. Sprint Retrospective
B. All Development Team members answering the three questions at the Daily Scrum
C. Sprint Burndown Chart
D. User Stories
E. All of the above

QUESTION 89

How much time is allowed between the conclusion of the current Sprint and the start of the next Sprint?

A. Maximum of one day for Sprints that are time-boxed to two weeks.
B. None. A new Sprint starts immediately following the conclusion of the previous Sprint.
C. Enough time for the last Increment to finish testing.
D. Enough time for the Product Owner to prepare the Product Backlog for Sprint Planning.
E. All of the above are allowed.

QUESTION 90

What are typical Product Owner activities during Sprint 0?

A. Creating a project plan based on the defined timeline.
B. Ensuring there is enough work to do for at least three Sprints.
C. Creating User Stories based on the requirements document.
D. Allocating enough resources before starting Sprint 1.
E. There is no such thing as Sprint.

Explanation:

There are no special Sprints. All Sprints are structured to produce potentially shippable product Increments.

QUESTION 91

A high performing Scrum Team will have frequent Release Sprints.

A. True
B. False

Explanation:

There are no special Sprints. All Sprints are structured to produce potentially shippable product Increments.

QUESTION 92

During the Sprint, the Development Team realizes they might not be

able to finish all of the items in the Sprint Backlog. What should happen?

A. Product Backlog items are either 'done' or 'not done.' This helps with transparency, reduces complexity and allows for improved empiricism.
B. Continue Sprinting until the work is complete and redefine a new Sprint time-box based on the results of the current Sprint.
C. The Sprint length holds and the Development Team continuously learns what is actually possible to do within the time-box.

QUESTION 93

Which statement is correct about the length of the Sprints?

A. All Sprints must be one month or less and it is optimal to have a consistent Sprint length.
B. The Sprint length is dependent on the development effort forecasted (amount of items selected) during Sprint Planning.
C. The Sprint length is calculated by aggregating the time required to design, code and test.
D. The Sprint Length is defined by the Scrum Master.

QUESTION 94

Who can prematurely cancel a Sprint?

A. The Development Team
B. The Product Owner
C. The Stakeholders
D. The Scrum Master

Explanation:

Only the Product Owner can determine when items being worked on are obsolete.

QUESTION 95

What must the Development Team do during the first Sprint?

A. Create a potentially shippable product Increment that includes at least one piece of functionality.
B. Analyze and estimate the requirements for the subsequent Sprints.
C. Create a project plan in order to map functional development to Sprint dates.
D. Only design and develop the architecture and infrastructure.

Explanation:

Sprints promote iterative and incremental development.

QUESTION 96

How should a Scrum Master respond if the Product Owner plans the first Sprint to only focus on setting up the infrastructure and architecture in order to work on functionality in a subsequent Sprint?

A. Help the Product Owner understand the value of including business functionality into every Sprint and explain to him/her that the best architecture and infrastructure emerge alongside the development of the functionality.
B. Support the Product Owner's decision as he/she is accountable for maximizing the value of the work that the Development Team does.
C. Explain that one Sprint may be too short to finish the architecture and he should pre-allocate subsequent Sprints just in case.
D. Add at least one technical architect to the Development Team to ensure the architecture can be completed in the first Sprint.

Explanation:

Getting feedback from the Users and Stakeholders is a crucial activity in Scrum. It reduces waste from building items that add no value. Saying that, the best architectures, requirements, and designs emerge from self-organizing teams.

QUESTION 97

The Sprint length should be:

A. Short enough to keep the business risk acceptable to the Product Owner.
B. Short enough to be able to synchronize the development work with other business events.
C. No more than one month.
D. All of these answers are correct.

QUESTION 98

When does a new Sprint begin?

A. Immediately after the next Sprint Planning.
B. Immediately after the end of the previous Sprint.
C. It depends on the Product Owner.
D. Every Monday.

QUESTION 99

When does a Sprint end?

A. When there is no work remaining in the Sprint Backlog.
B. When the time-box expires.
C. It depends on the Product Owner.
D. Immediately after the conclusion of the Sprint Review.

ANSWERS

1. Correct Answer: BD
2. Correct Answer: B
3. Correct Answer: CD
4. Correct Answer: ABE
5. Correct Answer: BCE
6. Correct Answer: B
7. Correct Answer: BCE
8. Correct Answer: F
9. Correct Answer: A
10. Correct Answer: D
11. Correct Answer: C
12. Correct Answer: B
13. Correct Answer: F
14. Correct Answer: A
15. Correct Answer: A
16. Correct Answer: B
17. Correct Answer: CD
18. Correct Answer: A
19. Correct Answer: A
20. Correct Answer: BCE
21. Correct Answer: CE
22. Correct Answer: AC
23. Correct Answer: B
24. Correct Answer: AC
25. Correct Answer: AD
26. Correct Answer: C
27. Correct Answer: BC
28. Correct Answer: C
29. Correct Answer: B
30. Correct Answer: A
31. Correct Answer: A
32. Correct Answer: B
33. Correct Answer: A
34. Correct Answer: C

35. Correct Answer: BEF
36. Correct Answer: AB
37. Correct Answer: B
38. Correct Answer: BCD
39. Correct Answer: A
40. Correct Answer: B
41. Correct Answer: C
42. Correct Answer: AD
43. Correct Answer: B
44. Correct Answer: AB
45. Correct Answer: A
46. Correct Answer: B
47. Correct Answer: B
48. Correct Answer: C
49. Correct Answer: A
50. Correct Answer: DE
51. Correct Answer: A
52. Correct Answer: B
53. Correct Answer: A
54. Correct Answer: B
55. Correct Answer: A
56. Correct Answer: C
57. Correct Answer: B
58. Correct Answer: B
59. Correct Answer: E
60. Correct Answer: D
61. Correct Answer: D
62. Correct Answer: B
63. Correct Answer: E
64. Correct Answer: D
65. Correct Answer: A
66. Correct Answer: D
67. Correct Answer: D
68. Correct Answer: A
69. Correct Answer: B
70. Correct Answer: C

71. Correct Answer: B
72. Correct Answer: A
73. Correct Answer: D
74. Correct Answer: B
75. Correct Answer: B
76. Correct Answer: A
77. Correct Answer: B
78. Correct Answer: B
79. Correct Answer: B
80. Correct Answer: B
81. Correct Answer: A
82. Correct Answer: E
83. Correct Answer: B
84. Correct Answer: C
85. Correct Answer: C
86. Correct Answer: A
87. Correct Answer: C
88. Correct Answer: A
89. Correct Answer: B
90. Correct Answer: E
91. Correct Answer: B
92. Correct Answer: C
93. Correct Answer: A
94. Correct Answer: B
95. Correct Answer: A
96. Correct Answer: A
97. Correct Answer: D
98. Correct Answer: B
99. Correct Answer: B

www.ingramcontent.com/pod-product-compliance
Lightning Source LLC
LaVergne TN
LVHW081804050326

832903LV00027B/2095